January 1970

Dick —
　　Let's Christmas in January!
　　　　Linda

Books by Robert Penn Warren

John Brown: The Making of a Martyr

Thirty-six Poems

Night Rider

Eleven Poems on the Same Theme

At Heaven's Gate

Selected Poems, 1923–1943

All the King's Men

Blackberry Winter

The Circus in the Attic

World Enough and Time

Brother to Dragons

Band of Angels

Segregation: The Inner Conflict in the South

Promises: Poems 1954–1956

Selected Essays

The Cave

All the King's Men (play)

You, Emperors, and Others: Poems 1957–1960

The Legacy of the Civil War

Wilderness

Flood

Who Speaks for the Negro?

Selected Poems: New and Old 1923–1966

Incarnations: Poems 1966–1968

Audubon: A Vision

Audubon

a vision

Robert Penn Warren

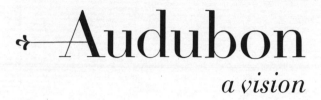

Audubon

a vision

Random House   New York

ACKNOWLEDGMENT
Parts of AUDUBON: A Vision *have previously been*
published in the following periodicals:
Harper's Magazine (*Part II*)
The New Yorker (*Parts* I A; IV A, C, E;
V A, B; VI; VII B)
The Yale Review (*Parts* I B; IV B, D; V C)

To Allen and Helen Tate

*Thou tellest my wanderings: put thou my tears
into thy bottle: are they not in thy book?*

—PSALMS: 56, 8

*I caught at his strict shadow and the shadow
released itself with neither haste nor anger. But
he remained silent.*

—Carlos Drummond de Andrade:
"Travelling in the Family"
Translated by Elizabeth Bishop

Contents

Audubon

a vision

Jean Jacques Audubon, whose name was anglicized when, in his youth, he was sent to America, was early instructed in the official version of his identity: that he was the son of the sea captain Jean Audubon and a first wife, who died shortly after his birth in Santo Domingo, and that the woman who brought him up in France was a second wife. Actually, he was the son of Jean Audubon and his mistress during the period when Jean Audubon was a merchant and slave-dealer in Santo Domingo, and the woman who raised him was the wife his father had left behind him in France while he was off making his fortune. By the age of ten Audubon knew the true story, but prompted, it would seem, by a variety of impulses, including some sound practical ones, he encouraged the other version, along with a number of flattering embellishments. He was, indeed, a fantasist of talent, but even without his help legends accreted about him. The most famous one—that he was the lost Dauphin of France, the son of the feckless Louis XVI and Marie Antoinette—did not, in fact, enter the picture until after his death, in 1851.

I   Was Not the Lost Dauphin

[A]

Was not the lost dauphin, though handsome was only
Base-born and not even able
To make a decent living, was only
Himself, Jean Jacques, and his passion—what
Is man but his passion?

                    Saw,
Eastward and over the cypress swamp, the dawn,
Redder than meat, break;
And the large bird,
Long neck outthrust, wings crooked to scull air, moved
In a slow calligraphy, crank, flat, and black against
The color of God's blood spilt, as though
Pulled by a string.

                    Saw
It proceed across the inflamed distance.

Moccasins set in hoar frost, eyes fixed on the bird,
Thought: "On that sky it is black."
Thought: "In my mind it is white."
Thinking: "*Ardea occidentalis*, heron, the great one."

Dawn: his heart shook in the tension of the world.

Dawn: and what is your passion?

[B]

October: and the bear,
Daft in the honey-light, yawns.

The bear's tongue, pink as a baby's, out-crisps to the curled tip,
It bleeds the black blood of the blueberry.

The teeth are more importantly white
Than has ever been imagined.

The bear feels his own fat
Sweeten, like a drowse, deep to the bone.

Bemused, above the fume of ruined blueberries,
The last bee hums.

The wings, like mica, glint
In the sunlight.

He leans on his gun.   Thinks
How thin is the membrane between himself and the world.

II   The Dream He Never Knew the End Of

[A]

Shank-end of day, spit of snow, the call,
A crow, sweet in distance, then sudden
The clearing: among stumps, ruined cornstalks yet standing, the spot
Like a wound rubbed raw in the vast pelt of the forest.   There
Is the cabin, a huddle of logs with no calculation or craft:
The human filth, the human hope.

                              Smoke,
From the mud-and-stick chimney, in that air, greasily
Brims, cannot lift, bellies the ridgepole, ravels
White, thin, down the shakes, like sputum.

                              He stands,
Leans on his gun, stares at the smoke, thinks: "Punk-wood."
Thinks: "Dead-fall half-rotten."   Too sloven,
That is, to even set axe to clean wood.

                              His foot,
On the trod mire by the door, crackles
The night-ice already there forming.   His hand
Lifts, hangs.   In imagination, his nostrils already
Know the stench of that lair beyond
The door-puncheons.   The dog
Presses its head against his knee.   The hand
Strikes wood.   No answer.   He halloos.   Then the voice.

[B]

What should he recognize?   The nameless face
In the dream of some pre-dawn cock-crow—about to say what,
Do what?   The dregs
Of all nightmare are the same, and we call it
Life.   He knows that much, being a man,
And knows that the dregs of all life are nightmare.

Unless.

Unless what?

[c]

The face, in the air, hangs.   Large,
Raw-hewn, strong-beaked, the haired mole
Near the nose, to the left, and the left side by firelight
Glazed red, the right in shadow, and under the tumble and tangle
Of dark hair on that head, and under the coarse eyebrows,
The eyes, dark, glint as from the unspecifiable
Darkness of a cave.   It is a woman.

She is tall, taller than he.
Against the gray skirt, her hands hang.

"Ye wants to spend the night?   Kin ye pay?
Well, mought as well stay then, done got one a-ready,
And leastwise, ye don't stink like no Injun."

[D]

The Indian,
Hunched by the hearth, lifts his head, looks up, but
From one eye only, the other
An aperture below which blood and mucus hang, thickening slow.

"Yeah, a arrow jounced back off his bowstring.
Durn fool—and him a Injun."   She laughs.

                                        The Indian's head sinks.
So he turns, drops his pack in a corner on bearskin, props
The gun there.   Comes back to the fire.   Takes his watch out.
Draws it bright, on the thong-loop, from under his hunter's-frock.
It is gold, it lives in his hand in the firelight, and the woman's
Hand reaches out.   She wants it.   She hangs it about her neck.

And near it the great hands hover delicately
As though it might fall, they quiver like moth-wings, her eyes
Are fixed downward, as though in shyness, on that gleam, and her face
Is sweet in an outrage of sweetness, so that
His gut twists cold.   He cannot bear what he sees.

Her body sways like a willow in spring wind.   Like a girl.

The time comes to take back the watch.   He takes it.
And as she, sullen and sunken, fixes the food, he becomes aware
That the live eye of the Indian is secretly on him, and soundlessly

The lips move, and when her back is turned, the Indian
Draws a finger, in delicious retardation, across his own throat.

After food, and scraps for his dog, he lies down:
In the corner, on bearskins, which are not well cured,
And stink, the gun by his side, primed and cocked.

Under his hand he feels the breathing of the dog.

The woman hulks by the fire.   He hears the jug slosh.

The sons come in from the night, two, and are
The sons she would have.   Through slit lids
He watches.   Thinks: "Now."

                                       The sons
Hunker down by the fire, block the firelight, cram food
Into their large mouths, where teeth
Grind in the hot darkness, their breathing
Is heavy like sleep, he wants to sleep, but
The head of the woman leans at them.   The heads
Are together in firelight.

He hears the jug slosh.

                       Then hears,
Like the whisper and *whish* of silk, that other
Sound, like a sound of sleep, but he does not
Know what it is.   Then knows, for,
Against firelight, he sees the face of the woman
Lean over, and the lips purse sweet as to bestow a kiss, but
This is not true, and the great glob of spit
Hangs there, glittering, before she lets it fall.

The spit is what softens like silk the passage of steel
On the fine-grained stone.   It whispers.

When she rises, she will hold it in her hand.

With no sound, she rises.   She holds it in her hand.
Behind her the sons rise like shadow.   The Indian
Snores.

      He thinks: "Now."

            And knows
He has entered the tale, knows
He has entered the dark hovel
In the forest where trees have eyes, knows it is the tale
They told him when he was a child, knows it
Is the dream he had in childhood but never
Knew the end of, only
The scream.

[G]

But no scream now, and under his hand
The dog lies taut, waiting.   And he, too, knows
What he must do, do soon, and therefore
Does not understand why now a lassitude
Sweetens his limbs, or why, even in this moment
Of fear—or is it fear?—the saliva
In his mouth tastes sweet.

"Now, now!" the voice in his head cries out, but
Everything seems far away, and small.

He cannot think what guilt unmans him, or
Why he should find the punishment so precious.

It is too late.   Oh, oh, the world!

Tell me the name of the world.

[H]

The door bursts open, and the travelers enter:
Three men, alert, strong, armed.   And the Indian
Is on his feet, pointing.

                    He thinks
That now he will never know the dream's ending.

Trussed up with thongs, all night they lie on the floor there.
The woman is gagged, for she had reviled them.
All night he hears the woman's difficult breath.

Dawn comes.   It is gray.   When he eats,
The cold corn pone grinds in his throat, like sand.   It sticks there.

Even whiskey fails to remove it.   It sticks there.

The leg-thongs are cut off the tied-ones.   They are made to stand up.
The woman refuses the whiskey.   Says: "What fer?"
The first son drinks.   The other
Takes it into his mouth, but it will not go down.

The liquid drains, slow, from the slack side of the mouth.

[J]

They stand there under the long, low bough of the great oak.
Eastward, low over the forest, the sun is nothing
But a circular blur of no irradiation, somewhat paler
Than the general grayness.   Their legs
Are again bound with thongs.

They are asked if they want to pray now.   But the woman:
"If'n it's God made folks, then who's to pray to?"
And then: "Or fer?"   And bursts into laughing.

For a time it seems that she can never stop laughing.

But as for the sons, one prays, or tries to.   And one
Merely blubbers.   If the woman
Gives either a look, it is not
Pity, nor even contempt, only distance.   She waits,

And is what she is,

And in the gray light of morning, he sees her face.   Under
The tumbled darkness of hair, the face
Is white.   Out of that whiteness
The dark eyes stare at nothing, or at
The nothingness that the gray sky, like Time, is, for
There is no Time, and the face
Is, he suddenly sees, beautiful as stone, and

So becomes aware that he is in the manly state.

[K]

The affair was not tidy: bough low, no drop, with the clients
Simply hung up, feet not much clear of the ground, but not
Quite close enough to permit any dancing.
The affair was not quick: both sons long jerking and farting, but she,
From the first, without motion, frozen
In a rage of will, an ecstasy of iron, as though
This was the dream that, lifelong, she had dreamed toward.

                                                          The face,
Eyes a-glare, jaws clenched, now glowing black with congestion
Like a plum, had achieved,
It seemed to him, a new dimension of beauty.

There are tears in his eyes.
He tries to remember his childhood.
He tries to remember his wife.
He can remember nothing.

His throat is parched.   His right hand,
Under the deerskin frock, has been clutching the gold watch.

The magic of that object had been,
In the secret order of the world, denied her who now hangs there.

He thinks: "What has been denied me?"
Thinks: "There is never an answer."

Thinks: "The question is the only answer."

He yearns to be able to frame a definition of joy.

And so stood alone, for the travelers
Had disappeared into the forest and into
Whatever selves they were, and the Indian,
Now bearing the gift of a gun that had belonged to the hanged-ones,
Was long since gone, like smoke fading into the forest,
And below the blank and unforgiving eye-hole
The blood and mucus had long since dried.

He thought: "I must go."

                         But could not, staring
At the face, and stood for a time even after
The first snowflakes, in idiotic benignity,
Had fallen.   Far off, in the forest and falling snow,
A crow was calling.

                     So stirs, knowing now
He will not be here when snow
Drifts into the open door of the cabin, or,
Descending the chimney, mantles thinly
Dead ashes on the hearth, nor when snow thatches
These heads with white, like wisdom, nor ever will he
Hear the infinitesimal stridor of the frozen rope
As wind lifts its burden, or when

The weight of the crow first comes to rest on a rigid shoulder.

III   We Are Only Ourselves

We never know what we have lost, or what we have found.
We are only ourselves, and that promise.
Continue to walk in the world.   Yes, love it!

He continued to walk in the world.

IV   The Sign Whereby He Knew

[A]

His life, at the end, seemed—even the anguish—simple.
Simple, at least, in that it had to be,
Simply, what it was, as he was,
In the end, himself and not what
He had known he ought to be.   The blessedness!—

To wake in some dawn and see,
As though down a rifle barrel, lined up
Like sights, the self that was, the self that is, and there,
Far off but in range, completing that alignment, your fate.

Hold your breath, let the trigger-squeeze be slow and steady.

The quarry lifts, in the halo of gold leaves, its noble head.

This is not a dimension of Time.

[B]

In this season the waters shrink.

The spring is circular and surrounded by gold leaves
Which are fallen from the beech tree.

Not even a skitter-bug disturbs the gloss
Of the surface tension.   The sky

Is reflected below in absolute clarity.
If you stare into the water you may know

That nothing disturbs the infinite blue of the sky.

[c]

Keep store, dandle babies, and at night nuzzle
The hazelnut-shaped sweet tits of Lucy, and
With the piratical mark-up of the frontier, get rich.

But you did not, being of weak character.

You saw, from the forest pond, already dark, the great trumpeter swan
Rise, in clangor, and fight up the steep air where,
In the height of last light, it glimmered, like white flame.

The definition of love being, as we know, complex,
We may say that he, after all, loved his wife.

The letter, from campfire, keelboat, or slum room in New Orleans,
Always ended, "God bless you, dear Lucy."   After sunset,

Alone, he played his flute in the forest.

[D]

Listen!   Stand very still and,
Far off, where shadow
Is undappled, you may hear

The tushed boar grumble in his ivy-slick.

Afterward, there is silence until
The jay, sudden as conscience, calls.

The call, in the infinite sunlight, is like
The thrill of the taste of—on the tongue—brass.

[E]

The world declares itself.   That voice
Is vaulted in—oh, arch on arch—redundancy of joy, its end
Is its beginning, necessity
Blooms like a rose.   Why,

Therefore, is truth the only thing that cannot
Be spoken?

It can only be enacted, and that in dream,
Or in the dream become, as though unconsciously, action, and he stood,

At dusk, in the street of the raw settlement, and saw
The first lamp lit behind a window, and did not know
What he was.   Thought: "I do not know my own name."

He walked in the world.   He was sometimes seen to stand
In perfect stillness, when no leaf stirred.

Tell us, dear God—tell us the sign
Whereby we may know the time has come.

V   The Sound of That Wind

[A]

He walked in the world.   Knew the lust of the eye.

Wrote: "Ever since a Boy I have had an astonishing desire
                  to see Much of the World and particularly
                  to acquire a true knowledge of the Birds of North America."

He dreamed of hunting with Boone, from imagination painted his portrait.
He proved that the buzzard does not scent its repast, but sights it.
He looked in the eye of the wounded white-headed eagle.

Wrote: ". . . the Noble Fellow looked at his Ennemies
                  with a Contemptible Eye."

At dusk he stood on a bluff, and the bellowing of buffalo
Was like distant ocean.   He saw
Bones whiten the plain in the hot daylight.

He saw the Indian, and felt the splendor of God.

Wrote: ". . . for there I see the Man Naked from his
                  hand and yet free from acquired Sorrow."

Below the salt, in rich houses, he sat, and knew insult.

In the lobbies and couloirs of greatness he dangled,
And was not unacquainted with contumely.

Wrote: "My Lovely Miss Pirrie of Oackley Passed by Me
this Morning, but did not remember how beautifull
I had rendered her face once by Painting it
at her Request with Pastelles."

Wrote: ". . . but thanks to My humble talents I can run
the gantlet throu this World without her help."

And ran it, and ran undistracted by promise of ease,
Nor even the kind condescension of Daniel Webster.

Wrote: ". . . would give me a fat place was I willing to
have one; but I love indepenn and piece more
than humbug and money."

And proved same, but in the end, entered
On honor. Far, over the ocean, in the silken salons,
With hair worn long like a hunter's, eyes shining,
He whistled the bird-calls of his distant forest.

Wrote: ". . . in my sleep I continually dream of birds."

*

And in the end, entered into his earned house,
And slept in a bed, and with Lucy.

                          But the fiddle
Soon lay on the shelf untouched, the mouthpiece
Of the flute was dry, and his brushes.

                              His mind
Was darkened, and his last joy
Was in the lullaby they sang him, in Spanish, at sunset.

He died, and was mourned, who had loved the world.

Who had written: ". . . a world which though wicked enough
                   in all conscience is *perhaps* as good
                   as worlds unknown."

So died in his bed, and
Night leaned, and now leans,
Off the Atlantic, and is on schedule.
Grass does not bend beneath that enormous weight
That with no sound sweeps westward.   In the Mississippi,
On a mud bank, the wreck of a great tree, left
By flood, lies, the root-system and now-stubbed boughs
Lifting in darkness.   It
Is white as bone.   That whiteness
Is reflected in dark water, and a star
Thereby.

      Later,
In the shack of a sheep-herder, high above the Bitterroot,
The light goes out.   No other
Light is visible.

The Northwest Orient plane, New York to Seattle, has passed,
                                        winking westward.

[c]

For everything there is a season.

But there is the dream
Of a season past all seasons.

In such a dream the wild-grape cluster,
High-hung, exposed in the gold light,
Unripening, ripens.

Stained, the lip with wetness gleams.

I see your lip, undrying, gleam in the bright wind.

I cannot hear the sound of that wind.

VI   Love and Knowledge

Their footless dance
Is of the beautiful liability of their nature.
Their eyes are round, boldly convex, bright as a jewel,
And merciless.   They do not know
Compassion, and if they did,
We should not be worthy of it.   They fly
In air that glitters like fluent crystal
And is hard as perfectly transparent iron, they cleave it
With no effort.   They cry
In a tongue multitudinous, often like music.

He slew them, at surprising distances, with his gun.
Over a body held in his hand, his head was bowed low,
But not in grief.

He put them where they are, and there we see them:
In our imagination.

What is love?

One name for it is knowledge.

VII   Tell Me a Story

[A]

Long ago, in Kentucky, I, a boy, stood
By a dirt road, in first dark, and heard
The great geese hoot northward.

I could not see them, there being no moon
And the stars sparse.   I heard them.

I did not know what was happening in my heart.

It was the season before the elderberry blooms,
Therefore they were going north.

The sound was passing northward.

[B]

Tell me a story.

In this century, and moment, of mania,
Tell me a story.

Make it a story of great distances, and starlight.

The name of the story will be Time,
But you must not pronounce its name.

Tell me a story of deep delight.

Robert Penn Warren

was born in Guthrie, Kentucky, in 1905. After graduating summa cum laude *from Vanderbilt University (1925), he received a master's degree from the University of California (1927), did graduate work at Yale University (1927–28) and then at Oxford as a Rhodes Scholar (B. Litt., 1930).*

A list of Mr. Warren's books appears in the front of this volume. The variety of forms is extraordinary, including eight novels, nine volumes of poetry, short stories, a play, critical essays, a biography, a historical essay, and two studies of race relations in America. This body of work has been published in a period of thirty-nine years—a period during which Mr. Warren also had an active career as a professor of English. He is now a member of the faculty of Yale University.

All the King's Men (1946) was awarded the Pulitzer Prize for fiction. Promises (1957) won the Pulitzer Prize for poetry, the Edna St. Vincent Millay Prize of the Poetry Society of America, and the National Book Award. In 1944 Mr. Warren occupied the Chair of Poetry of the Library of Congress. In 1959 he was elected to the American Academy of Arts and Letters. In 1967 he received the Bollingen Prize in Poetry for Selected Poems: New and Old 1923–1966.

Mr. Warren lives in Connecticut with his wife, Eleanor Clark (author of Rome and a Villa *and* The Oysters of Locmariaquer), *and their two children, Rosanna and Gabriel.*